CAVES

By Ronal C. Kerbo
With Photographs by the Author

A Radlauer Geo Book

AN ELK GROVE BOOK

 CHILDRENS PRESS, CHICAGO

To my wife and children with love

For help with the manuscript, the author thanks
Patty Fry, Ruth Radlauer, and Michael Queen, Ph.D.,
Tulane University of Louisiana.

Cover:
A New Mexico Cave
Photo credits:
Andy Galewsky, page 30 (top)
Dan Lenihand, page 30 (bottom)

**Created for Childrens Press
by Radlauer Productions, Incorporated**

Library of Congress Cataloging in Publication Data

Kerbo, Ronal.
  Caves.

  (A Radlauer geo book)
  "An Elk Grove book."
  Includes index.
  Summary: Discusses how caves are formed and what
a spelunker might find while exploring a cavern.
    1. Caves—Juvenile literature.   [1. Caves.
2. Speleology]   I. Title.   II. Series: Radlauer
geo book.
GB601.2.K47   910'.02'144   81-4514
ISBN 0-516-07638-8   AACR2

CONTENTS

If you want to look at the world from the mouth of a cave, you need training to do it safely.

WHAT IS A CAVE?

When you hear the word "cave" what do you think about? Dark? Scary? Bats? Snakes?

Maybe you think about people called **spelunkers** or **cavers**. Have you ever met one of them? Do you know what they do?

Come on then, and as you read this book, see if you can find the answers to these questions. Find out if caves are dark and scary. Find out if caves have bats and snakes. Find out who these spelunkers are and what they do.

After you learn about caves you may want to visit one. The best way to see a cave is to visit one of the many **developed caves** in the United States. If you go to a **wild cave**, be sure you go with an expert spelunker. Then remember what spelunkers say. "Take only pictures, and leave only footprints."

spelunker
    person who explores caves
caver
    another name for *spelunker*
developed cave
    cave with electric lights and man-made trails
wild cave
    undeveloped cave with no lights or trails

Caves form in limestone rock, which is
one kind of sedimentary rock.

THE ROCKS

A long, long time ago, when the earth was young, it looked different. Some places that are now land were under oceans, and some places that are now under oceans were dry land.

Billions of tiny animals that lived in the oceans died and sank to the bottom. They piled up in thick layers and were slowly covered with **sediment** from rivers that ran to the sea. After millions of years, the bodies of the animals and sediment layers got heavier and heavier. The tremendous weight caused them to turn into rock.

Still later, earth movements caused the rocks to rise. The waters drained away and left dry land and the mountains of today. Those little animals and the sediment have become a kind of rock called **sedimentary** rock. **Limestone** is one kind of sedimentary rock.

sediment
matter that settles to the bottom of a liquid
sedimentary
formed by or from deposits of sediment
limestone
rock formed of sediment; consists mainly of shells and coral

7

Even though you can't see them, this canyon contains many caves beneath its limestone layers.

THE LAND

The earth movements that created the mountains also caused cracks to form. These cracks, called **fractures** and **joints**, helped create caves.

The kind of country where caves form is called **karst**. This word comes from Karst, an area in Yugoslavia where there are a lot of caves in limestone. Now **geologists** call all cave country by that name.

Karst country is found just about everywhere on earth. Every state in the U.S. has caves. Some states, like Missouri and Kentucky, have a lot. Others, like Kansas or Rhode Island, have only a few.

Caves are found inside mountains, under deserts, and beneath cities like San Antonio, Texas. Do you live in karst country? Are there any caves where you live? To find out, ask if there is any limestone nearby.

fracture
    break or crack
joint
    space between two surfaces
karst
    land that has caves, underground rivers, and springs
geologist
    scientist who studies the history of the earth as recorded in rocks and landforms

The sign reads:

LINCOLN
National Forest

HIDDEN CAVE

THIS CAVE WAS STARTED MILLIONS OF YEARS AGO BY PERCOLATING GROUND WATERS WHICH DISSOLVED PORTIONS OF THE LIMESTONE.
IT IS PROTECTED AND MANAGED FOR YOUR ENJOYMENT. DAMAGE OR REMOVAL OF ANY CAVE FORMATIONS IS PROHIBITED.

PLEASE

"TAKE ONLY PICTURES, LEAVE ONLY FOOTPRINTS"

FOR ADDITIONAL INFORMATION, CONTACT
GUADALUPE DISTRICT RANGER
FOREST SERVICE
CARLSBAD, NEW MEXICO

U.S. DEPARTMENT
OF AGRICULTURE

Sometimes signs at a cave entrance explain its formation and tell how to protect this special place.

THE CAVE

The earth is covered with soil and plants. A gas called **carbon dioxide**, CO_2 for short, is produced by dead and decaying plants. Rainwater picks up CO_2 as it soaks downward into the ground. Water with CO_2 in it becomes a weak **acid** called **carbonic acid**.

This acid water goes deep into the earth through fractures and joints in the rock. As the water travels downward, it dissolves part of the limestone and carries it away in **solution**. After a very long time, water eats away tons of rock and forms a cave.

Sometimes the rock dissolves very close to the surface of the earth. If the surface breaks, a cave entrance is formed. The entrance may be a deep pit or one you can walk into. If water runs into the entrance, an underground river may start to flow.

carbon dioxide
> (CO_2) gas formed by decaying plants; odorless, colorless gas used in soft drinks

acid
> sour, sharp to the taste; a compound that reacts with a substance by eating it away

carbonic acid
> weak acid; water plus CO_2

solution
> liquid containing a dissolved substance

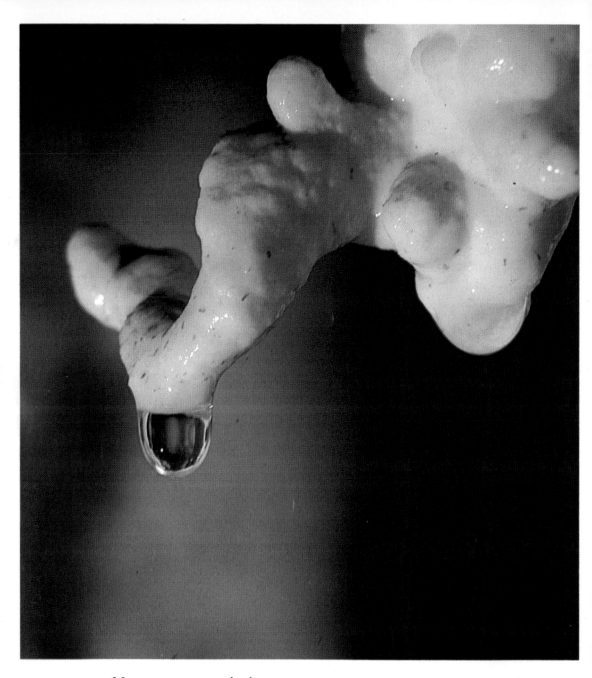

Here you see a helictite, a cave
speleothem that grows in all directions.

CAVE DECORATIONS— SPELEOTHEMS

In a cave, you may have seen **speleothems** hanging from the ceiling and sticking up from the floor. These limestone decorations are called **stalactites** and **stalagmites.** Some others are called **helictites.**

Speleothems are formed by water. Remember that limestone is in solution in the water. As water seeps into a cave, it clings to the ceiling in little drops. The CO_2 comes out of the water the same way bubbles leave soda pop. Without CO_2, limestone can no longer stay in solution.

As each drop of water loses CO_2, a little ring of limestone is **deposited** on the cave ceiling. This happens over and over again until a hollow tube is formed. After a long time, this tube becomes a stalactite, hanging from the ceiling.

Drops of water also leave limestone deposits on the floor. These deposits slowly build up into stalagmites.

speleothem
  limestone decoration in a cave
stalactite
  speleothem that hangs from a cave ceiling
stalagmite
  speleothem that builds up from a cave floor
helictite
  odd-shaped speleothem that "grows" in all directions; twisted, spiral formation
deposit
  to lay down or leave behind; material left behind, like a bathtub ring after the tub is drained

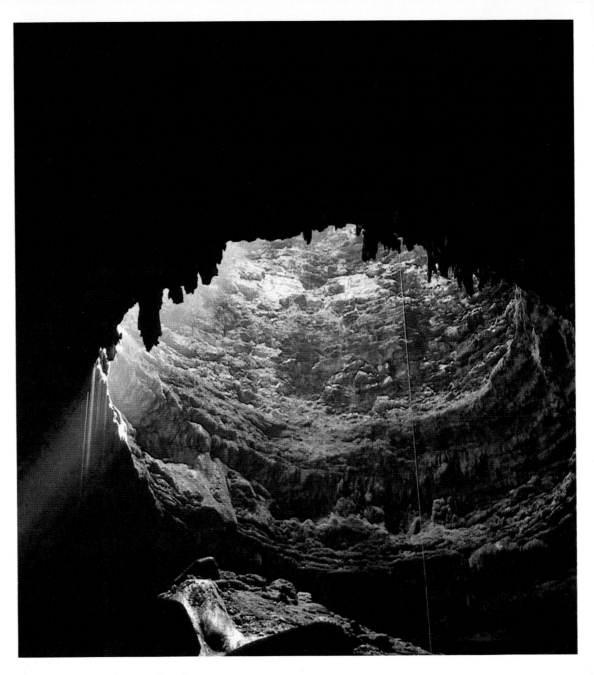

Sunlight shines into a cave entrance.
This is the twilight zone of a cave in Texas
called the Devils Sinkhole.

THE TWILIGHT ZONE

The part of a cave where sunlight can reach is called the **twilight zone**. Some animals use the twilight zone of a cave. Ringtailed cats go in and out hunting for mice. Cave swallows build mud nests in **cavern** entrances. You can also find mice, rats, snakes, porcupines, and skunks in and around caves.

The twilight zones of some caves were also used by Indians. These areas provided shelter from wind, rain, or desert sun. Scientists have found evidence of Indian use of the caves. Some of the things they have found are burnt rocks from fires, broken pottery, arrowheads, and paintings on the walls called **pictographs**.

twilight zone
> area near the entrance of a cave that receives light from the sun

cavern
> cave

pictograph
> painting on rock

A cave is like a stone desert.

THE DARK ZONE

What about the part of the cave that is always dark? The animals that live there are very special. There is not much to eat in a cavern. It is all rock, and animals don't eat rock.

You could call a cave a stone desert. Large animals, like bears or mountain lions, could not live in the **dark zone** of a cave. Such large animals need a lot of food.

Since plants cannot grow in the darkness of a cave, almost all the food must crawl in through the entrance or be carried in by an underground river. Sometimes bats bring food into a cave.

The dark zone, then, is a world without sun, a world filled with the sound of dripping water. It is a place with very few animals and very little food: a stone desert.

dark zone
    part of a cave where no light from the sun can reach

In the evening, a group of insect-eating bats fly out of Carlsbad Cavern in New Mexico.

BATS AND CRICKETS

Some animals like bats love the twilight zone and the dark zone of caves. Bats are **mammals** like bears, coyotes, and you. As a bat flies in the dark, it finds its way by making sounds with its nose and mouth. Echoes of the sounds help the bat know where to fly. Echoes also tell the bat when a moth or insect goes by. Then the bat catches the insect in its wing and transfers it to its mouth.

You may have heard that bats are blind. They are not, nor will they fly into your hair. Most of the bats in the United States are quite small with a **wingspan** of about 25 to 30 centimeters. All but one kind of bat in the U.S. are insect eaters. The one that does not eat insects is a nectar-feeder like a hummingbird.

Cave crickets are not blind either, and like bats, they come out of the cave at night to feed. They are very pale in color and have long **antennae** that help them find their way around in a dark cave.

mammal
　　hairy, warm-blooded animal that gives live birth and feeds its young milk from the mother's body

wingspan
　　measurement from one wing tip to the other

antennae
　　jointed horns or feelers on insects' heads

A cave fish has no need for eyes. This blind fish is from a cave in the mountains of Mexico.

TROGLOBITES

Are there animals in caves that are blind and white? Is it true? Yes, in most caves there are solid white or pale pink animals that have no eyes, and never come out of the darkness. They are called **troglobites**.

Troglobites live in total darkness, so they have no use for eyes. They get around by feel and smell. They are white because their skin needs no colored layer to protect them from the sun's rays. These special animals have **adapted** to living in caves. They could not live very long outside of a cave.

Some troglobites you might see in a cave are salamanders, fish, and crayfish. There are also spiders, mites, and some kinds of insects. If you shine a light on a troglobite it will try to get away. It can feel the heat from the light and will not like it. Seeing a troglobite in a cave is a special treat.

troglobite
  cave dweller; specially adapted animal that lives in a cave's dark zone and nowhere else
adapt
  to change or adjust to an environment

The entrance to Carlsbad Cavern, a
very famous cave in New Mexico.

FAMOUS CAVES

Carlsbad Cavern and Mammoth Cave are two very famous caves. They are safe and easy for you to visit. Since they are both in national parks, you can go through them with guides. Carlsbad and Mammoth have lights in them and trails to walk on.

Some other famous developed caves are Caverns of Sonora, Texas; Jewel Cave, South Dakota; Howe Caverns, New York; and Lewis and Clark Caverns in Montana.

The longest cave in the world is Flint-Mammoth-Joppa in Kentucky. The deepest cave in the world is Jean Bernard Cave in France. The deepest cave in the United States is Great Ex Cave in Wyoming. The deepest cave in North America is a **cave system** in Mexico.

cave system
    two or more caves connected by small or hard-to-find passages

These cavers don't worry about mud.
They're just excited about the wonders they
have seen in a New Mexico cave.

CAVERS

Who are the people that explore caves? Where do they come from? What do you call them?

Those who explore caves are called cavers or **spelunkers**. They can be bus drivers, nurses, beekeepers, or teachers. They are young, old, short, or tall. Just about any sort of person can be a caver.

There are many reasons why people cave: the thrill of finding new cave passages and rooms, taking photographs, or mapping caves. There are even artists who take their paints and **canvas** into caves.

Cavers enjoy mountains, the out-of-doors, and deep caverns to explore. Most of them would rather be caving than doing anything else. After a good trip, they enjoy telling each other what they did and saw in the caves. Then they start thinking about their next caving trip.

spelunker
    person who explores caves
canvas
    cloth on which artists paint

While mapping a cave the caver must crawl through mud and still keep paper and pencils clean.

MAPPING A CAVE

There are people who love to map caves. They say you don't really know a cave until you have made a map of it. They may be right, but it sure is a lot of trouble.

Caves are not easy to map. You can't see very far, equipment has to be small, and sometimes mud gets all over the **transit**. Note paper gets wet, pencil lead breaks, and tape measures can get tangled up on rocks.

Once the **survey** work is finished in the cave, there is still more to be done. Transit sights and distances are transferred onto a computer which corrects them. Taking the survey notes as a guide, the caver uses **drafting** tools to start drawing the shape of the cave. That's also a lot of work. Don't forget your pencil sharpener!

transit
> compass used for surveying

survey
> to determine size by measuring distances and angles

drafting
> drawing a map, plan, or sketch

Speleologists use a transit and tape to map a cave.

SPELEOLOGISTS

Going into caves for sport is fun, but there are people who cave for science instead of sport. They are the **speleologists**. They enjoy caverns as much as anyone else, even though they may have their noses pressed close to a rock studying some strange troglobite or speleothem.

Most of our knowledge of caves has come from the work of speleologists. Some of them study only cave animals, others study the **geology** of caves. There are speleologists who study underground rivers, because people who live in karst country get their drinking water from these rivers.

One French speleologist spent six months alone in a Texas cave. He never knew if it was day or night outside the cave. His study helped **NASA** understand the effects of people being alone in space.

speleologist
> scientist who studies caves and their relation to the rest of the earth

geology
> study of the earth, its rocks, and landforms

NASA
> National Aeronautics and Space Administration; a government agency that runs the space program

Getting into a cave to dive can be hard
work. It's a sport for experts.

CAVE DIVING

Some caves in Texas and Florida are full of water. When cavers want to explore these places they have to use **scuba** diving gear. They use air tanks, **regulators**, underwater lights, masks, and fins. As they swim, they unroll long reels of line so they can find their way back out of the cave.

This kind of diving is very specialized and should never be attempted without a lot of training. In underwater caves you cannot come straight up to the surface if you get into trouble. You must return the way you came in. Cave divers wear waterproof watches and check them often, so they will not stay in the caves too long and run out of air.

Cave divers have explored miles of underwater passages. Experts know cave diving can be dangerous and always follow strict safety rules. The first rule is to leave cave diving to the experts.

scuba
> self-contained underwater breathing apparatus; the diver's air supply

regulator
> valves and rubber hoses on scuba tanks through which a diver breathes

Cavers need rock climbing skills. These young people learn to rappel before trying it in a cave with an expert caver.

HOW TO BE A CAVER

Walking, crawling, climbing, **rappeling**, diving! People do all these things just to explore a cave? Yes, these and more. If you want to explore caves, begin by visiting a developed cave. Then find out if anyone you know is a caver and let that person teach you.

Beginning cavers start with easy caves and then go on to more difficult ones. They never go alone and always go with more experienced cavers. Rope work and climbing techniques are practiced outside before trying them in a cave.

You can find out if there is a caving club in your area by writing to the **National Speleological Society**. Also some scouting groups take trips into caves.

rappel
> to go down a steep rock with the aid of a rope; also a controlled slide down a rope

National Speleological Society
> caving club—The address is:
>> Cave Avenue
>> Huntsville, Alabama 35810

For safety, this caver wears a hard hat
with an electric light.

A CAVE TRIP—
EQUIPMENT

We are ready now to meet some cavers and go on a cave trip. Before we go into a wild cave, we'll tell someone where we're going and when we plan to be back. Then if anything happens to us, they'll know where to send help.

Cavers always wear hard hats, old clothes, and good boots. The hard hat has a light attached to it. It may be a small **carbide** lamp or a battery-powered light.

A caver always carries a pack with at least two extra lights in it. The pack will also contain other things like water, candy bars, matches, first aid supplies, and spare parts for the lights. Depending on the kind of cave being explored, a caver may take ropes and climbing gear or scuba equipment.

carbide
    grey, pebblelike substance mixed with water to create a
    gas that can be burned to make a flame like a candle's

These cavers are still in the twilight zone
of a cave, getting their equipment ready
before they go deeper.

GOING IN

The cave we are going to visit is in the desert mountains of New Mexico. It is hot outside the entrance but it will be cool in the cave. Hear the chirping? Those are cave swallows. Up there in that small hole is the nest of a great horned owl. At night an owl may feed on bats.

Do you see or hear any rattlers? Further in, you won't see any snakes, because snakes only use the cave entrance as a place to get out of the hot sun.

Feel it getting cooler? We're in the twilight zone now. Near the ceiling you can see the mud nests of cave swallows. Once away from the sunlight we will have to turn on our lights to see the cave.

Be careful on the steep slope of rocks that piled up here when the entrance fell in thousands of years ago. The rocks could be loose and cause you to fall.

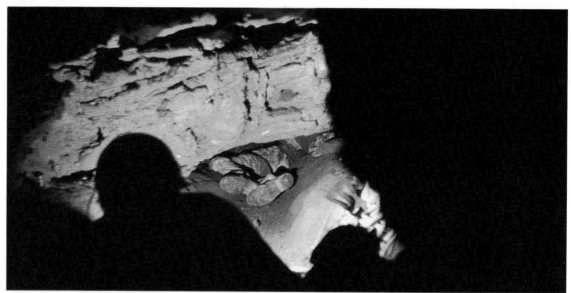

Cavers climb up through tight passages to find things like these beautiful wet stalagmites.

EXPLORING

O.K. All lights on? As we go back into the dark, the ceiling gets lower. The rock feels cool and rough to our hands. Now the ceiling is so low we have to crawl and water is flowing into our **crawlway** from another passage. The cave is cold and getting muddy.

Look, we are coming to a big room. As we wiggle out of the crawl and stand up we see our first stalagmites. They are wet and shiny with water. We'd better not touch them with our muddy hands. The ceiling is a forest of stalactites. See the water drops reflecting your light?

Be careful of the **rimstone dams** on the floor. If you step on them, they will break. We'll walk around the pools so we won't stir them up and make the water muddy.

Look out! There's a pit. It must be 20 meters deep. We'll only look down into it this time. You can explore pits after you've done more caving and learned to rappel.

crawlway
> (**crawl** for short) small space through which a caver must crawl to get somewhere

rimstone dams
> ridges of limestone deposits on a cave floor that look like dams on a river

When you're leaving a cave, the sky
always looks *especially* blue.

LEAVING THE CAVE

Our trip is over and it is time to return to the entrance. We can't go any farther and we have been here quite awhile. Let's get going so our friends at home won't worry about us. Isn't it good to realize that someone knows we're in a cave?

We'll go back through the big room, and into the crawl. Then we'll go through the little stream flowing through this narrow passage. Ahead we can see the entrance light.

The blue sky and white clouds are really different from the grey rock and white speleothems of the cave. Notice the different sounds. Outside we hear birds and wind. Inside there was only the sound of dripping water, the whisper of the stream, and the echoes of our voices.

If you enjoyed your cave trip and want to see more, be sure to do it safely by going with expert cavers. Most cavers think the earth and all that is under it is a very special and friendly place. Remember when you go into a cave, "Take only pictures, leave only footprints, and kill nothing but time."

These draperies in a wild cave in New
Mexico are 10 meters long.

CAVE RULES

1. Never cave alone.
2. Always tell someone where you are going and when you expect to be back.
3. Always carry three lights.
4. Never try anything beyond your abilities.
5. Always go with more experienced people.
6. Be an expert scuba diver before going for cave-diving instruction.
7. Take only pictures, leave only footprints, kill nothing but time.
8. Remember that caves are a very special environment that can be easily damaged.
9. Have fun.

These rules will help you get started. You can learn more about safety, conservation, and the fun of caves from expert cavers and by reading other **books about caving.**

books about caving
Gans, Roma, *Caves*
Laycock, George, *Caves*
Radlauer, Ruth, *Carlsbad Caverns National Park*
——*Mammoth Cave National Park*

GLOSSARY

acid
sour, sharp to the taste; a compound that reacts with a substance by eating it away

adapt
to change or adjust to an environment

antennae
jointed horns or feelers on insects' heads

canvas
cloth on which artists paint

carbide
grey, pebblelike substance mixed with water to create a gas that can be burned to make a flame like a candle's

carbon dioxide
(CO_2) gas formed by decaying plants; odorless, colorless gas used in soft drinks

carbonic acid
weak acid; water plus CO_2

cave system
two or more caves connected by small or hard-to-find passages

caver
another name for *spelunker*

cavern
cave

crawlway
(**crawl** for short) small space through which a caver must crawl to get somewhere

dark zone
part of a cave where no light from the sun can reach

deposit
to lay down or leave behind; material left behind, like a bathtub ring after the tub is drained

developed cave
cave with electric lights and man-made trails

drafting
drawing a map, plan, or sketch

fracture
break or crack

geologist
scientist who studies the history of the earth as recorded in rocks and landforms

geology
study of the earth, its rocks, and landforms

helictite
odd-shaped speleothem that "grows" in all directions; twisted spiral formation

joint
space between two surfaces

karst
land that has caves, underground rivers, and springs

limestone
rock formed of sediment; consists mainly of shells and coral

mammal
hairy, warm-blooded animal that gives live birth and feeds its young milk from the mother's body

NASA
National Aeronautics and Space Administration; a government agency that runs the space program

National Speleological Society
caving club—The address is Cave Avenue, Huntsville, Alabama 35810.

pictograph
painting on rock

rappel
to go down a steep rock with the aid of a rope; also a controlled slide down a rope

regulator
valves and rubber hoses on scuba tanks through which a diver breathes

rimstone dams
ridges of limestone deposits on a cave floor that look like dams on a river

scuba
self-contained underwater breathing apparatus; the diver's air supply

sediment
matter that settles to the bottom of a liquid

sedimentary
formed by or from deposits of sediment

solution
liquid containing a dissolved substance

speleologist
scientist who studies caves and their relation to the rest of the earth

speleothem
limestone decoration in a cave

spelunker
person who explores caves; see *caver*

stalactite
speleothem that hangs from a cave ceiling

stalagmite
speleothem that builds up from a cave floor

survey
to determine size by measuring distances and angles

transit
compass used for surveying

troglobite
cave dweller, specially adapted animal that lives in a cave's dark zone and nowhere else

twilight zone
area near the entrance of a cave that receives light from the sun

wild cave
undeveloped cave with no lights or trails

wingspan
measurement from one wing tip to the other

INDEX

THE AUTHOR

Ronal Kerbo first became interested in caves in 1967 when he and a friend found a small cave. He has been exploring caves ever since. He began scuba diving in 1959 and cave diving in 1968.

Ronal is a member of the Cave Research Foundation and the National Cave Rescue Commission. He is presently employed by the National Park Service as the Cave Specialist for Carlsbad Caverns and Guadalupe Mountains National Parks. He lives in New Mexico with his wife and three children.